Prolance

www.prolancewriting.com
California, USA
©2018 Natalia Nabil
Illustrations ©2018 Melani Putri
ISBN: 978-0-9996991-4-0

Muslim Girl, Growing up
A guide to puberty

By Natalia Nabil
Art by Melani Putri

PROLANCE

Dedicated to:

the blossoms of my life; my daughters
Mernan and Layan who inspired me to
write this book for them and for every
young Muslim girl out there.

Table of Contents

Introduction:

One weekend morning, I was sitting drinking my coffee while my daughter was sitting in front of me playing with her iPad. I was staring at her face for a long time and kept remembering her features as a little baby. Suddenly I realized that my little baby isn't a baby anymore, in just one month she would turn the big 10. After just one month my small butterfly will say good-bye to childhood and will enter a new stage of her life — Puberty. I immediately left my coffee and went to sit beside her. I gave her a big hug and told her how much I loved her and that I couldn't believe how big she was getting. Time was flying by. After that, I kept thinking and realized that a lot of changes are headed her way, and that there is a lot information she will need to be taught about the changes that will happen to her body and life so that there are no surprises.

So I thought to myself, "How can I prepare her for this new phase?" I wanted to find a resource that can explain to her the details of this special stage while also integrating the important aspects of it from the Islamic religion. Being from the West, most books I found only explained the physiological changes. But I found that Muslim girls, especially ones from Western countries, need to know more about the religious implications of this stage.

So I decided to write this guide to help young girls understand the basic things a Muslim girl should know about puberty, including the religious aspects that come along with it.

However, this guide is just a starter to the journey ahead. I encourage parents to talk with your teens and pre-teens about this important stage of life to have a full and thorough understanding.

Chapter 1: WHAT IS PUBERTY?

Puberty is a very special stage that every girl will pass through. It is the transition from childhood to adolescence.

It can start as early as 8 years old for some girls and sometimes as late as 15 years old.

The majority of girls will hit puberty around age 12. It ends when your body takes its final shape at around age 17.

Before puberty, your family takes care of your physical well being. For the most part, every detail about your body is your family's responsibility. But now, you will have to start taking responsibility for the cleanliness and upkeep of your own body.

The Prophet Mohamed
(peace be upon him) said that,
"Cleanliness is a symbol of faith."

Chapter 2: STAGES OF PUBERTY

Stage 1

(8-11 years old): At this stage the ovaries in your body begin to enlarge. The ovary is one of the organs in the female body that is responsible for reproduction, or creating babies, and also for producing female hormones. Externally there are no noticeable or visible changes in the body.

PUBERTY CAN BE SPLIT INTO 5 PHYSIOLOGICAL STAGES.

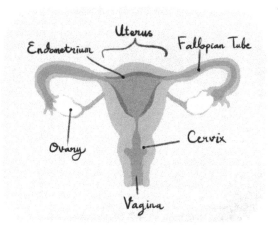

Stage 2

(8-14 years old): This stage begins with some initial signs that are visible. This includes the growth of breasts and nipples. Also there is an increase of the dark area surrounding the nipple. Pubic hair also starts to appear. It can be coarse and curly or light and soft. This stage also can have over-all weight gain and increased height.

Stage 3

(9-15 years old): During this stage your breasts will continue to grow. Pubic hair will also increase. There may be an appearance of white vaginal discharge in your underwear and when you go to the bathroom. Finally, menstruation (or period) may start.

Stage 4

(10-16 years old): In this stage, there may be an increase in the visibility of the nipple and the brown area surrounding it. Your period will start, if it has not already. Ovulation starts at this stage as well. When ovulation begins, this means that the body is able to become pregnant.

Stage 5

(12-19 years old): In this final stage of growing the body reaches its final height, regular ovulation, pubic hair and breast growth completeness.

Chapter 3: MENSTRUATION

The most significant thing that happens to any girl during puberty is the beginning of her period.

It is a natural phenomenon.

The period is an amount of blood that comes out of the uterus in the form of red liquid and stays from 3 to 7 days. With most girls, the period comes every 22-28 days. So about once a month. But it's different from girl to girl. Don't be worried if you find your friend's cycle different than your own in how long it stays or how long in between each period.

Also, at the beginning of puberty, it is very normal that your cycle is irregular. It is common for it to come once then skip a month or two. The body usually needs up to two years to regulate the period.

The Prophet Mohamed
(peace be upon him) said to Aisha,
"It is something that Allah prescribed to
all of Adam's female children."

First Day!

When that day comes that you find out you've gotten your first period, it will announce itself by a bright red or dark brown stain in your underpants. It can happen anywhere and at anytime. Wherever you are, even if you are not at home with your parents, you should find a responsible adult like a teacher, the school nurse, or another family member to tell.

There is no need to be shy about it!

All you have to say is, "I think I just got my period," and let them help you. If you are at school, there will be supplies, like pads, for these occasions and they will give you one to use. If you don't know how to use it don't be shy to ask for directions.

What if you are only with your friends? If that happens tell a friend that you know has already gotten her period. Ask her if she has an extra pad. If not, then go to the restroom and wipe yourself as well as you can, fold up a wad of toilet paper or tissues to put into your underwear until you are back home.

SUPPLIES!

Deciding which kind of pad to use is simpler than you might think. You can buy a small pack of each kind to try in the first couple

of months. After a while you will figure out which one is most comfortable for you.

Most brands now have scented and unscented pads. The scented ones have perfumes and other chemicals to fight odors in the pad caused by fluids, but sometimes, for some girls, the scented ones irritate skin and can cause an allergic reaction. It might be better to use the unscented kinds and keep yourself clean and fresh by changing the pad regularly.

Types of pads:

*Regular pads: They look thin but they are very absorbent, they can be used any time during your period, though if your flow is heavy, you will need to change your pad more often. *Maxi pads: Used to be big but now they look almost as thin as regular pads but are more absorbent. These are good to use in the very heavy flow days and to sleep at night. *Pads with wings: Now most of the pads with all sizes have wings, the wings are an extra material on the edge to prevent leaking fluids in your underpants. *Panty liners: These are very thin and smaller than the other kinds. Most girls like to wear them at the end of their period. Some girls wear them even if they don't have their period, because they don't like the feeling of every-day vaginal discharge.

15

CHANGING YOUR PAD:

Since you are a big girl now you should take care of your personal hygiene. During your period you must take extra care of your cleanliness. You should change your pad often because the blood that comes out during your period makes a bad odor sometimes. So it's a good idea to change it about every two hours or whenever there is blood in the pad. Before you sleep take a warm shower and change your pad then change it again first thing in the morning.

DISPOSING YOUR PAD:

Also, be sure to dispose your pad in a right way. Whether you are at home or outside never throw it away in the toilet. You can wrap the old one in the new outer wrapping of the new pad by rolling it up or wrapping the old pad in toilet paper and putting it in a trash.

How to know when it's over:

Once your period becomes regular, which can take up to two years, you can tell how long it stays with you. It starts with heavy bright red blood then trickles down at the end and turns from bright red to brown.

But sometimes the blood flow can stop for several hours then come back. But if there is no blood for up to two days that means the period is over.

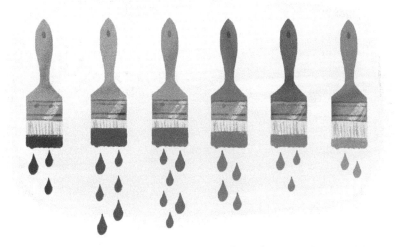

Once your period is over:

During your period a girl does not perform her daily prayers. When your period is over, a Muslim girl must make "ghusl." Ghusl is an Arabic word, which means washing the full body. It is a necessary ablution before you can start praying again.

Special note:
Girls who have braids should undo them before doing ghusl so that the water touches and washes all of her hair.

Steps for Ghusl:

According to some scholars:
1. Make the internal intention to perform it.
2. Say Bismillah.
3. Wash the right hand up to and including the wrists. Make sure to rub between the fingers too. Make sure no part of the hand is left dry. Three times. Then do the same with the left hand. Also, three times.
4. Wash your private parts. Three times.
5. Swirl water in the your mouth and spit it out three times.
6. Rinse the nose by sniffing in a little water then blowing it out. Three times.
7. Wash the face three times, from the hairline to the jawbone and chin, and to the ears.
8. Wash the right arm up to and including the elbow. Three times. The arm extends from the fingertips, including the nails, to the lower part of the upper arm. It is essential to remove anything stuck to the hands before washing them, such as dough, mud, paint, nail polish etc, that could prevent the water from reaching the skin. Do the same with the left arm. Three times.
9. Pour water over the head three times down to the roots of your hair, rubbing the roots of the hair with wet fingers.

10. Pour water over the entire body, beginning with the right side and then the left side. Then pour water over your head. (Ensuring that no part of the body is untouched by water by rubbing the body with your hands).

11. Wash the right foot up to and including the ankles, the sole, the heals, and between the toes. Three times. Wash the left foot in the same manner as the right foot. Three times.

12. Then say the following Duaa: *Ashhadu an laa ilaaha ill-Allaah wahdahu laa shareeka lah, wa ashhadu anna Mohamed rasool Allah.* (I bear witness that there is no god except Allah alone, with no partner and I bear witness that Mohamed is His Messenger.)

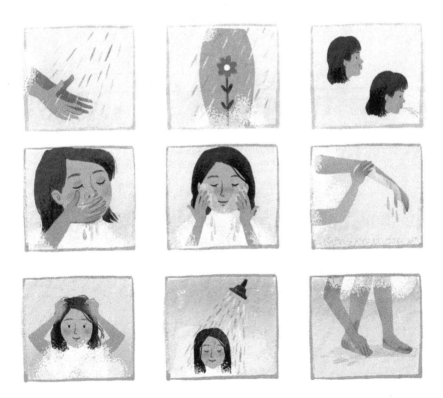

Chapter 4: WHAT YOU NEED TO KNOW (OR DO OR NOT DO) DURING YOUR PERIOD

PRAYING:

According to Islamic teachings, you should stop praying during your period. Why? Because during your period you do not have purity - full cleanliness, which is the most important condition to pray.

The Prophet Mohamed (peace be upon him) said, "Prayer is not accepted without purification."

In other words, while a girl is on her period you are constantly, uncontrollably, secreting unclean blood so it is impossible to remain purified.

FASTING:

Scholars have also come to the conclusion that a woman should not fast during her period because when they body is in menstruation it is weak. And when you are feeling weak or sick you should not fast.

Your body needs water and food for nourishment during this time. When you're on your period you should eat healthy and drink a lot of fluids all day.

The goal of fasting is for worship, not to cause any pain.

So in Ramadan a girl usually misses about one week of fasting because of her period. Those missed days should be made up later in the year. You can choose to fast the missed days in a row or a day each week or each month...any way you feel comfortable but you should finish them before the next Ramadan if you can.

QURAN:

Some scholars also believe you should try not to touch the Quran. But, just because you shouldn't touch it doesn't mean that you cannot recite it from what you have memorized or from a phone or tablet.

PMS:

Once your period begins to be regular you may notice some changes in how you feel right before your period. These changes could be physical or emotional changes and sometimes both together.

Those changes are called premenstrual syndrome or PMS. It is just a natural part of the menstrual cycle. It is caused by hormones (chemicals that are released in your body at this time). The changes you feel can be a clue for when your period is about to start so you can be ready for it. Around a week before your period starts you may feel some of these changes.

They can include: swollen or tender breasts, heaviness, puffiness, cramps in lower abdomen or back, and headache. These signs are very normal and most will go away after your period begins.

Also, your period can affect your mood. Some girls are very emotional and over-sensitive at this time. You may also experience a lack of energy. Some are grouchy and easily irritated. Some girls like to eat more sweets or more salty foods.

It's important to take care of yourself during this time!

You can try things like getting rest, maybe listen to music, take a walk, or write in a journal. You should find your own way to feel better. There are many remedies for premenstrual discomfort as well. There are medications at the drugstore that you can try. Talk to an adult and ask which medications are safe. You can also try natural remedies like exercise, a warm bath, or warm water bottle over your tummy. Also swimming is a great way to relax your body.

Don't forget to eat healthy! Eat plenty of fruits and vegetables and drink a lot of fluids especially water and cut down on salty foods because salt makes your body retain water.

Chapter 5: HYGIENE

...ss is a sign of good faith in Islam, so you have to take care of your hygiene. Here are some tips!

UNDERARMS:

Your underarms are the area in your body that sweats the most. When the underarms are not clean the bacteria mixes with sweat on your skin and makes a bad smell. So make sure you are bathing regularly especially after a long day at school or playing sports. It is a good idea to take a quick shower daily before going to bed.

Once you wash your underarms you should use an underarm product that helps keep odor away called deodorant.

Another sign of puberty is having hair under your arms. You can discuss with your parent when and how is a good way to remove it.

HAIR:

As you get older your hair may start getting more oily. So you may need to wash regularly and if you are playing sports you may have to wash it daily after your exercise. You can try out different shampoos till you find the best one for your hair type.

As you take care of your hygiene make sure to also take care of the tools you use to do so. For example your hair brush should always be clean. You can wash it with water and mild soap at least once every ten days. And don't forget; you should not share your personal hygiene tools with others.

The ears are easy to take care of. Each time you take a shower you just need to give them a good dry with a towel or cotton swab. You should never ever put anything pointy into your ear, it can cause serious damage to your ear drum. If you go swimming at the pool a lot, make sure you clean your ears after. Sometimes the pool water is not clean and that can cause ear infections. It's an even better idea to use earplugs.

Ear piercings:

Some do it when their child is a newborn, or around one years old, and some don't pierce at all. Others leave the decision to the girl herself when she's older. If you have a new piercing, first allow at least two months for the hole to heal before you can change your medical earrings.

Clean your newly pierced ears daily with rubbing alcohol to avoid any kind of infection but if you feel any kind of itching or redness you must tell an adult. If your skin is very sensitive try to avoid accessories that are not made out of gold or silver.

26

MOUTH:

Your nice smile is the first impression people have of you. You must take good care of your mouth by brushing your teeth after each meal and flossing at least once a day. Floss comes in waxed or unscented, thick or thin varieties. Remember, the remaining food in between your teeth can make a bad smell in your breath. Brushing your teeth is not only for your teeth's health but also to give you fresh breath, which is important for social reasons.

Special note:

While fasting - your breath might be a little stale because you didn't eat or drink for a long time.

The same as when you wake up after 8 or 9 hours of sleep. To avoid bad breath while fasting you can wash your teeth in the morning carefully without swallowing any water or toothpaste or use mouth wash carefully. If you feel you might swallow any just rinse your mouth every couple of hours instead.

Chapter 6: YOUR PRIVACY

You must know that your body is yours and yours alone. No one else has the right to deal with it in any way, not even family.

It is your right to take care of yourself the way you find comfortable. If anyone touches you in a way you don't like, you must tell your parents or someone responsible right away.

It is not necessary to protect the person who is causing you to be uncomfortable.

Also, when a girl or boy reaches the age of puberty they become responsible for their actions in the eyes of Allah. So make sure you are acting with righteousness, always.

Always try to be a good role model as a Muslim girl at your school and with your friends and family!

CPSIA information can be obtained
at www.ICGtesting.com
Printed in the USA
BVHW090811020222
627770BV00010B/866